Meditation Made Easy

Meditation Made Easy

BY W. P. PETERSEN
illustrated by Terry Fehr

FRANKLIN WATTS
NEW YORK | LONDON | TORONTO | 1979

Library of Congress Cataloging in Publication Data

Petersen, W   P
Meditation made easy.

(A Concise guide)
Includes index.
SUMMARY: Discusses the techniques and benefits
of meditation, a state of consciousness known as
"deep rest." Also suggests exercises designed to
help beginners enter this state.

1. Meditation—Juvenile literature. [1. Meditation]
I. Fehr, Terrence. II. Title.
BL627.P47   158'.1   79–11812
        ISBN 0–531–02894–1

Contents

What is Meditation?

Every morning at about 9:30, a business executive closes the door to her office. Her secretary, familiar with this routine, knows that she will receive no calls for the next ten minutes. She sits down in the leather chair in front of her mahogany desk and closes her eyes. For ten minutes she doesn't move. Occasionally, her head nods up and down. Her eyes open briefly once or twice for glimpses at her watch. When ten minutes have gone by, she slowly opens her eyes, sits for another minute or two, and then turns her attention to the work on her desk.

It would seem that the executive has fallen into the habit of grabbing a little extra sleep every morning. But in fact, she has joined millions of other people all over the country, and indeed the world, in a regular habit of meditation. The executive is not alone. All kinds of people—truck drivers, business people, teachers, students, doctors, and factory workers—are meditating on a regular basis.

Why are so many people spending twenty minutes or more a day meditating? There are almost as many answers to that question as there are meditators. Whatever the reasons, meditation of one kind or another has gained tremendous popularity since the 1960s.

To many observers, meditation may seem to be the newest and latest fad. But there is actually nothing new about it. People have been meditating for thousands of years. Although meditation is taught as a technique, it can come quite naturally if we let it happen.

But just what is meditation? According to *Webster's Dictionary,* to meditate is "to reflect upon or muse over; to intend or ponder; to engage in contemplation or reflection." This is not very helpful, is it? In fact, it is actually misleading.

The words *reflect* and *contemplate* describe an action. They suggest that the meditator is *doing* something. Other synonyms, such as *speculate, brood, cogitate, reason,* or *deliberate,* suffer from the same failure. They also suggest that the meditator is actively *doing* something.

Meditators themselves will insist that they are doing *nothing,* thinking *nothing.* For them, meditation is a state of mind where the person meditating simply *is,* and nothing more. But this definition is not very helpful either. It is too negative. It merely tells us what meditation is not.

Perhaps the easiest way to define it is to say that meditation is a *dwelling upon* something, not the act of *thinking about* it. Take, for example, a candle flame. The longer you gaze at it, the more your mind will merely dwell upon it without thinking about it. After a while, you will begin to feel that you are *at one* with the flame. Through meditation you experience a oneness in all things and all beings which cannot be experienced through the five senses.

This point is beautifully expressed in an old story of an elephant in a city of blind men. In the story, the populace became anxious to see the elephant, and sightless people ran like fools to find it. Since they did not even know the form or shape of the elephant, they groped sightlessly, gathering information by touching some part of it. Each thought he knew about the animal, because he could feel a part of it.

When they returned to their fellow citizens, eager groups clustered around them. Each of these was anxious, misguidedly, to learn the truth from those who were themselves astray.

The man whose hand had reached an ear was asked about the elephant's nature. He said, "It is a large, rough thing, wide and broad like a rug." And the one who had felt the trunk said, "I have the real facts about it. It is like a straight and hollow pipe, awful and destructive." The one who had felt its feet and legs said, "It is mighty and firm, like a column."

Each had felt one part out of many. No mind knew all. All imagined something, something incorrect."

Any definition of meditation is like the elephant in this story. Perhaps the only real way to understand meditation is to experience it yourself.

A NEW STATE OF CONSCIOUSNESS?

To many people, the word *meditation* conjures up visions of monks and religious mystics sitting for hours doing nothing more than staring into space. Meditators will insist that meditation and its benefits are by no means the exclusive property of mystics or reclusive monks. In fact, they maintain that just the opposite is true. The techniques and benefits of meditation are available to anyone.

Recent scientific research by psychologists and physiologists indicates that meditation may be a totally separate state of consciousness. Up to about twenty years ago it was thought that there were only two states of consciousness, one experienced when we are asleep; the other, while awake. In recent years brain wave measurements and other tests have provided strong evidence that dreaming is a third state of consciousness. Similar evidence indicates that meditation could well be a fourth state of consciousness.

It is, of course, obvious that we reap enormous benefits from sleep. And there is ample evidence that we benefit from dreaming. People who are kept from dreaming become irritable and complain of feeling tired all the time. A great deal of research on the effects of meditation has been done in recent years. This research has produced an immense amount of evidence that meditation may indeed have many physical as well as psychological benefits.

There seem to be as many benefits from meditation as there are meditators. People have always claimed they obtained many positive results from meditating. In the past, such claims could not be verified. Today, however, the scientific evidence in favor of the health benefits of meditation is building. So before we go into the *how* of meditation, let's investigate the *who* and *why*.

Why Meditate?

Is meditation bad for some people? Who can benefit the most from meditation? Why even bother?

Meditation, done properly and not in excess, is not bad for you, or anyone for that matter. It is true, however, that the wrong person sometimes tries the wrong technique. When this happens, rest assured that no lasting damage has been done.

As pointed out before, all kinds of people are meditating. In general, people who feel they are constantly under pressure claim to find relief from that pressure through meditation. The meditator achieves a state of alertness along with relaxation. Not only do people who meditate perform better during moments of crises, but continued practice with meditation enables them to achieve a level of restful alertness at all times. Because of this fact they are also able to recover more quickly from tense situations.

Tests have been made in which people were kept from sleeping for long periods of time. This experience produces great stress in them, as anyone might expect. Since dreaming is thought to be a form of release from tension, measurements were made of the experimentors' dreams when they were finally allowed to sleep. These measurements showed that the nervous systems of those who were in the habit of meditating recovered more quickly from the lack of sleep than happened with the non-meditators.

Another benefit of meditation is that it reduces anxiety and increases your control over your own body and mind. Changes in the chemistry of the blood are one indication of anxiety which have been used in experiments with students. Without exception, students who meditate have been shown to have less anxiety and tension than students who did not meditate.

Another experiment, conducted at the University of Texas, showed that meditators have faster reflexes than do people who do not meditate. An equal number of meditators and non-meditators were tested. All were college students of about the same age and academic level. When asked to press a key on cue, the meditating students were 30 percent faster and more accurate in their responses. This result, the researchers contend, was because the people who did not meditate became tense. The meditators, on the other hand, remained in a state of restful alertness, and were able to react with more accuracy.

Among the other mental benefits attributed to meditation are the ability to increase your attention span and concentration. This means you can think harder and for a longer period of time without being distracted.

Have you ever lain awake on the night before a big test only to fall asleep at your desk the next day? These tense situations are a major cause of insomnia. People were tested to see if any real improvement resulted from meditation. It was found that meditation relaxed the basic body rhythms and made them more stable. Subjects found relief from their insomnia after only a short period of practice. And, with meditation, there are no bad side-effects as there can be with sleeping pills. In addition, they found that the people who meditated were able to get along with less sleep.

MEDITATION AND LEARNING

Because there are so many mental benefits, some people ask if meditation will increase their intelligence. The answer is no. What meditation *will* do is increase your ability to realize the full powers of your intelligence. This will allow you to respond to situations more quickly, with greater understanding and imagination.

As a result of learning to meditate, you will learn to use more of your abilities and use them more effectively. Meditation is a valuable aid to your normal study habits. It can bring about a general improvement in your mind as well as your nervous system. As a result, your school grades are likely to improve.

Tests have been made which show that meditation will enable you to perform better at any effort, including school work. With better performance, you will become more productive. And, when your work becomes more productive, you will become more satisfied with yourself.

Meditation and the Body

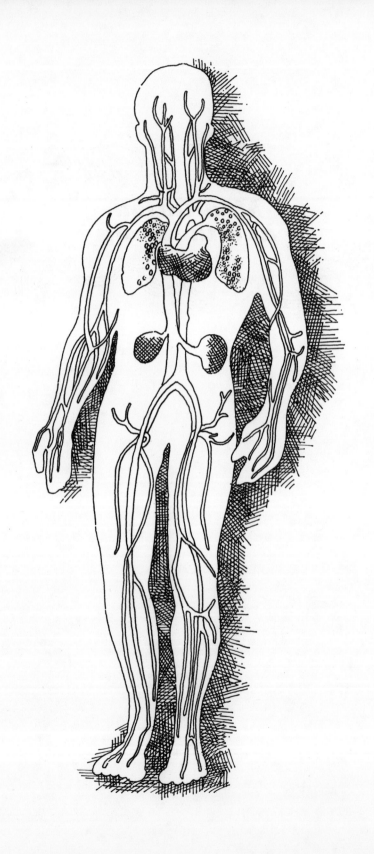

The mind is an astonishingly complex and mysterious entity which has defied understanding by scientists and doctors for thousands of years. No one has yet weighed or measured a thought. No one has ever seen or touched an idea. No one knows the full answer to what goes on in those 13,000,000,000 cells of the brain that weigh only about 3 pounds (1.36 kg).

But medical science has been able to measure the body. And in the last twenty years doctors have begun to acquire a better understanding of the brain. When medical investigators got around to researching meditation and its effects on the body, they found some truly astounding alterations. In this chapter we will explore what science knows about meditation. One thing can be said at the outset: medical researchers have found substantial proof that meditation does significantly alter the way brain and body function.

Of the many life-support systems contained in our body, none is more important than the complex network of arteries, veins, and capillaries. These run throughout the body, beginning and ending with the heart. Blood is continuously circulated by this ever-beating heart in what is properly called the cardio-vascular system.

Two rather simple tests can give us a fair picture of how the cardiovascular system is working. One is the measurement of the pulse, and the other is the measurement of blood pressure, or the pressure exerted by the blood against the walls of the arteries.

People in developed countries in the West suffer from a wide variety of ailments connected with the cardiovascular system. We have a high death rate due to heart attacks and strokes, and a large percentage of people with elevated cholesterol which constricts the blood vessels. It seems that people are forever in a hurry, always on the go. All this running around and agitation leads to what doctors call "stress" and psychiatrists call "anxiety." Either of these two problems can lead to a disease called hypertension.

Stress and anxiety lead not only to troubles with the cardiovascular system, but are contributing factors in such ailments as asthma, ulcers, and epilepsy, to name just a few.

The early warning signs of too much stress and strain show up when a doctor takes the patient's blood pressure and pulse rate. High blood pressure is an indication of constricted blood vessels, an overworked heart, or hypertension.

One of the first clues that meditation had something to offer came when it was found that people who meditated regularly had lower blood pressure readings and slower heartbeats when compared to non-meditators who were roughly the same age and held the same types of jobs. What amazed the investigators, however, was that during meditation the pulse rate and blood pressure of the person dropped dramatically. The decline in both readings was so dramatic that the doctors were puzzled. The readings looked very much like the readings doctors had come to expect in people who were asleep. In a few cases the readings even dropped below those of ordinary sleepers.

Another indication that meditation altered bodily functions came when it was discovered that a person deep in meditation drastically reduced his or her consumption of oxygen. Other, more sophisticated tests, continued to show that meditation could and did change the way the body operated. Even the blood's chemistry showed substantial changes during meditation. Left without a term for these curious body functions; the scientists decided to call the meditating state "deep rest."

MEDITATION AND THE BRAIN

The researchers went farther and conducted electronic tests with a device called an electroencephalograph, or EEG for short. An EEG monitors and records the tiny electrical currents of the brain and displays the various activity in a series of tracings called "brain waves." Over the years four basic types of brain waves have been identified with specific mental activity. They are:

Delta waves, which are long, slow, and lazy waves, all thought to be the exclusive property of infants, who spend eighty per cent of their sleep time producing them. Delta waves usually disappear by the age of five.

Theta waves are very special waves produced during dreams or periods of intense mental activity which the test subjects invariably report to be highly creative.

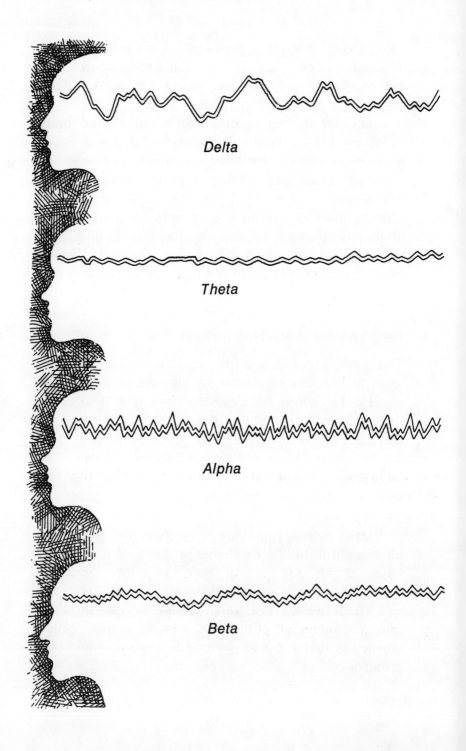

Delta

Theta

Alpha

Beta

Alpha waves are produced by people who are awake but not involved in anything specific. Alpha waves usually mean the mind is feeling peaceful. Alpha waves (named Alpha because they were the first waves discovered) have come to be associated with restful alertness.

Beta waves are produced when the brain is involved in complex reasoning. Puzzle solving, or concentration on difficult tests bring on Beta waves, which indicate that the brain is functioning at peak capacity. Beta waves are also produced when people are suffering from chronic anxiety or stress.

Test results consistently showed that people adept at meditation seemed capable of producing Alpha waves at will and, more importantly, sustaining these "pleasure waves" for long periods of time.

During the course of a day all of us, at one time or another, meditator or non-meditator, produce any one of the last three waves. At any time Alpha, Beta, and sometimes Theta waves may creep into our tracings. It is important to remember that anyone can produce these different waves. People who meditate, however, demonstrate an ability to *control* the electrical activity of the brain.

Through all these tests, researchers concluded that people who meditated clearly experienced lower levels of stress and anxiety. The importance of this conclusion lies in the fact that stress and anxiety are believed to be two major causes of illness and unhappiness in the Western World today.

Is meditation a cure for all cardiovascular ailments? No. In fact, relying on meditation and ignoring sound medical advice is a sure road to disaster. But, through these tests, meditation has proved itself to be a useful tool in maintaining a healthy mind and body.

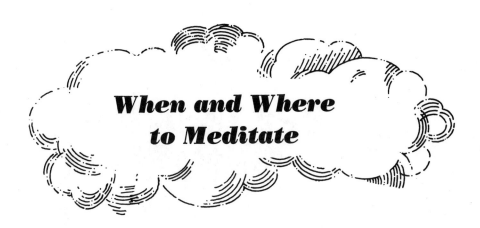

When and Where to Meditate

"Every journey begins with a single step," is an old Chinese proverb about good beginnings. If ever there was a journey that required a good start, it is the trip into meditation. As easy as meditation is to learn, a bad beginning will ruin the best-intended efforts of a novice venturing into the unknown.

Necessary for a good start is a reasonable schedule to follow. Deciding how often and at what times to meditate is a personal matter, but it is an important one. Obviously, you don't want to set up a schedule for yourself that is impossible to maintain. But, like anything that takes practice, regularity is important in order to progress. Therefore, you have to consider most carefully the matter of when to meditate.

Of the many different approaches to meditation, there are several that specify exact times. A Muslim, for example, is instructed to set aside five periods a day for reflection and prayer. For most other people who meditate, however, meditating twice a day is most convenient. On the two-a-day schedule, you may reserve ten minutes each morning and ten minutes each evening. This seems to be a good approach whether you are going to school, working at an outside job, or working at home. People with odd schedules have to select their own times, but there are some general rules to follow.

Meditating directly after meals is not a good idea. Meditation seems to slow down body functions—including digestion.

There is rarely time at school or work to stop for ten minutes without interruption, so trying to set aside time during the day is often not a good idea either. It might be interesting for you to know that certain American companies have generously provided rooms for their employees' use at personally convenient times. These "meditation rooms" have been widely accepted and utilized by grateful employees.

Another poor time to meditate is when you know someone is going to interrupt you, or when you're expecting a phone call. In both of these cases, your mind is not going to cooperate with even your best effort.

You may be wondering about combining the two ten-minute sessions into one twenty-minute session. This is not usually a good idea. Prolonged meditation, like anything in excess, has many disadvantages. If it comes down to one session and one session only, stick with the ten-minute time limit. But before you leap at this chance to get out of half the work, let's look at some of the reasons for trying to work out a twice-daily schedule. The most obvious reason of all is that morning and night come around with a high degree of reliability. That may sound funny but the truth is people have an inner sense of time that is dependent on the predictable progress of day into night. We all have this biological clock. Another good reason for having two meditation periods is that you approach each session with a different energy level and get more or less from your meditation because of it. In the morning, for example, you are refreshed from a good night's sleep (hopefully), and after waking up can get into your morning session with full confidence that you will not nod off. (A word about falling asleep during meditation: If it happens, let it. You probably needed the rest anyway.)

After a day at school or work, you may find you need a bit more discipline for the evening session. But you don't want to be over-tired, so don't put off your evening meditation until after the late news. You have to have some strength left.

The biggest problem about the *where* part of meditation is finding a place you can depend on day after day, twice a day at the same time. A place where interruptions and responsibilities will leave you alone for ten minutes.

A person with his or her own bedroom and a fixed school or work schedule will have an easy time setting up a regimen. If you live with your family, and quiet, private space is at a premium, it may be difficult to pick two periods each day for meditation. An understanding, fully-informed family can be a great help when it comes to close quarters.

People have been known to meditate in the oddest places imaginable. Fire escapes, elevators, roofs, garages, the family car, or the basement can all offer the quiet and solitude necessary for meditation. Some extremists go to improbable lengths for just the right setting. One man was known to meditate in his son's tree house.

Let's assume for now that you have your own room that happens to be ideal for meditating. You leave for school every day at 7:30 A.M. after getting out of bed at 7:00. Every afternoon, you come home to your room that contains a comfortable chair (a firm bed will do, but a chair is better), a clock that is easy to look at, a phone that can be taken off the hook, and fantastic parents who are enthusiastic about meditation. Okay, we've got the *where* worked out. Now how do you make the time?

First, of all, you get up earlier. This isn't as tough as it sounds. People who meditate regularly report that they need less sleep. All right. Up at 6:45.

It's not a good idea to roll out of bed and into a chair in order to meditate. You're supposed to be awake. A trip to the bathroom, perhaps a glass of juice, then back to your room. After ten quiet minutes you're back on schedule and off to school on time.

When you walk back into the house after school there may be chores or housework to do. It's best to get them out of the way so they won't be on your mind.

Okay. Now it's 5:15 P.M. and dinner is forty-five minutes away. Up to your bedroom, close the door, slip into a comfortable posture, and in ten minutes you're back downstairs with plenty of energy to enjoy the evening.

By now you should have a pretty good idea about how to go about suiting the *where* and the *when* of meditation to your own lifestyle. Now you're ready to learn how.

How to Meditate

Now you are ready to actually begin meditating. You will find that some approaches to meditation are easy while others are much more difficult. Don't think that one approach is better because it is more difficult. No one approach to meditation is "the best." Each approach is different, and should be suited to the individual. Only your own experience will tell you which method is most natural and easy and most satisfying for you.

THE PATH TOWARD UNION

These exercises are designed to convey the experience of meditation in various ways. If you are a visual person who enjoys looking at the world around you, you will probably be attracted to one type of meditation. If you are interested in poems and music, you may find another meditation technique more to your liking. If you go in for athletics, still another. In these exercises, there is something for almost everyone.

What is important is that you learn to experience the unity between your mind and body. Think of your mind as a walkie-talkie which can be tuned to receive and send messages to the world around you. Think of your body as the battery which makes it work.

THE THREE BASIC FORMS
OF MEDITATION

At first, you may find there is a confusing variety of methods. Some types of meditation want you to meditate with ideas; others insist on your abandoning all ideas. Some emphasize mental images; others discourage all such images. Some methods involve awakening your five senses; others emphasize a complete withdrawal from the senses. Some call for sitting still; others involve dancing.

However, there is a unity underneath this diversity. Regardless of how meditation is carried out, the attitude of the meditator is basically the same. All types of meditation have one trait in common. All meditation is a *dwelling upon* something.

In most of our daily life, our minds flit from one thing to another. The body moves from posture to posture. Meditation involves trying to stop this wasted mental and physical activity. With consistent meditation, you will learn to focus your energy and increase your concentration. You will find this will make you more efficient and effective at whatever you choose to do.

All the bewildering forms of meditation may be grouped under three headings: The Way of Concentration, The Way of Awareness, and The Way of Negation. But before you begin any of these forms of meditation, some preliminary warming up is necessary.

Situate yourself in a quiet room, and sit comfortably in a chair, on a bed, or on the floor. For the first few seconds or minutes, let your eyes stay open and gaze at some convenient object. One of your hands will do—but don't think about it, just *see* it. (And don't think about just seeing it either.) Then let your eyes close and relax without attempting to meditate. Having gazed prior to closing your eyes, your mind will be more or less free of thoughts. Try to be aware of the feeling of your body relaxing.

Tension usually manifests itself in muscular contraction. To overcome this tension, assume a passive attitude and attempt to still the flow of images through your mind. These images produce almost unnoticeable tensions in the muscles of the face and body.

Now, imagine a feeling of heaviness in your limbs. Focus your mind on the feeling of warmth creeping through your legs and arms. Become aware of your breathing but keep it calm and natural. Finally, relax each muscle in your body. Start with your eyebrows, mouth, and eyes. Drop your head and let it swing slowly back and forth. Do this several times to relax the muscles in your neck. Then move on to your shoulders, arms, and hands. Now your stomach muscles, and finally, your legs.

It is important to repeat this session of mental and physical relaxation before and after each exercise. After you do, you are ready to begin meditating. Let us begin with The Way of Awareness.

The Way of Awareness

THE FIRST DAY (MORNING)

Sit down and cross your legs so that your ankles rest easily under your calves. Sit up straight, as though someone were drawing you up by your hair. This position enables the energy within you to flow up and down your spine to your brain. Now place your hands on your thighs, palms open and turned up, so that energy can flow into your hands. Relax your hands. This is a modified Lotus Position.

Focus your entire awareness on your breathing. Breathe normally for a few minutes. Feel the air as it flows through your nostrils and into your lungs. Listen to the sound your breath makes. Now extend your awareness to your heart and feel it beating inside you.

When you feel ready, breathe in while you count to five slowly. Hold your breath for the same count of five. Then breathe out, counting again to five. Repeat this exercise about ten times. Keep your attention entirely on your breathing.

We normally breathe at a rate of sixteen times a minute. As you enter deeper into meditation, your breathing will slow down to ten or even eight times a minute. Finish this and each exercise with relaxing and gazing as outlined on page 30.

THE FIRST DAY (EVENING)

Assume the Lotus Position. Imagine that your body is a battery, charging and discharging energy. Tense your arms until you can feel your muscles vibrate. Then relax and let the energy flow out of you. Do the same thing with your stomach muscles and then with your legs. Now repeat the exercise, tensing all the muscles in your body four or five times.

Breathe in to the count of five as you slowly tense your muscles. Hold your breath and keep your muscles tense for another count of five. Relax and breathe out to the same count. When you are holding your breath and tensing your body, you should feel as if you are vibrating like a violin string when a bow is drawn across it.

Throughout both these exercises, try to keep your awareness focused entirely on your breathing and the way your body feels. Do not let your mind think of anything else.

THE SECOND DAY (MORNING)

Assume the Lotus Position or relax comfortably in a chair. Close your eyes. Do nothing with your body or mind or will—just look, keeping your eyes closed. After a few moments, different shades of lights will begin to appear in patterns. These patterns are caused partly by light coming through your eyelids. But the main cause is the rapid movements of your eyes, even though you are unconscious of your eyes moving at all.

Just look at the lights moving behind your eyes. Don't think about anything. Don't try to form them into patterns. They will continue to change shape and hue and formation. Like clouds, they will occasionally even form themselves into vaguely realistic pictures. Don't try to make them do anything; just watch them change.

THE SECOND DAY (EVENING)

Repeat the above exercise. But this time look beyond the patterns of light. Focus your attention on the darkness beyond these patterns. That darkness is one of the gateways to the Core of Energy, from which your awareness comes. Dwell upon that darkness. See if you can feel a deep calmness come over you. Stay with that feeling and keep your awareness focused on the darkness.

Slowly, let your mind drift out of the darkness. Let your awareness drift back to the lights, to your heart beating, to your breathing. And open your eyes.

THE THIRD DAY (MORNING)

Now that you are beginning to develop a greater awareness of your body, you are ready to increase your mental awareness. Remember, awareness is an art, like painting a picture or playing a musical instrument. Your native ability must be developed by regular practice and applying yourself. With time and hard work, you will find that a greater awareness extends to every moment of your life. Certainly that achievement is worth a little effort. Let us begin with an exercise that will develop your mental awareness.

Look around the house and find an old wooden pencil. Examine it carefully. Before you read any further, make a list of everything you were aware of as you examined the pencil. Finish your own list before you compare it with the one below.

(37)

Details of an old wooden pencil:

A. Shades: (1) Point—dark gray lead; (2) Metal eraser casing—brass with circular and stipped indentations around it; (3) Eraser—dark red with smudges of black and gray; (4) Lettering—with indentations painted black; (5) Shaft—painted yellow, chipped with teeth marks and the bare wood showing through; (6) Wooden part of the point—many shades of a brownish red.

B. Shapes: (1) A cone-shaped point; (2) Lead tip blunted with use; (3) Metal eraser-casing—ribbed and perforated; (4) Eraser—worn to many levels and little corners; (5) Shaft—six-sided, about 6 inches (15 cm) long.

C. Materials: (1) Wood; (2) Lead; (3) Rubber; (4) Flecks of dirt; (5) Paint—yellow and black; (6) Brass.

D. Distinguishing Marks: (1) Round point; (2) Trademark: Kenmore; (3) Lead quality—Number 3; (4) Brand name and number—A. W. Faber, #3; (5) Quality control number—205; (6) Made in U.S.A.; (7) Many chips, mostly teeth marks.

E. Possible Uses: (1) Writing; (2) Drawing; (3) Erasing; (4) Stirring; (5) Weapon; (6) Fuel (wood for burning).

This is only a partial list of things that can be said about a pencil. See how many more you can think of. Your powers of awareness will increase by leaps and bounds as you focus your whole attention on one subject at a time.

THE THIRD DAY (EVENING)

Repeat the exercise of this morning. Use something simple, a common household object like a fork, knife, cup, glass, or mirror. It's best to wait a few weeks before you meditate on a complicated object such as a flower.

THE FOURTH DAY (MORNING)

Close your eyes and imagine that you are floating in a warm, blue ocean. Hold this feeling in your mind. Now smell the salt air blowing over you. Taste the salt water on your lips. Hear the sound the ocean makes in your ears. Gaze at the blue ocean of light above you. Imagine that you are floating gently up and down like a wave. Feel the water relaxing you until there is no difference between you and the ocean.

The purpose of this exercise is to bring each of your senses into your awareness. Begin with imagining the feeling of warm water around your body. Think only of that feeling. Then think only of how the ocean smells and add that sensation to the first one. Continue with each of your senses. Try to imagine all five of your senses working at once. Don't be discouraged if you are able to recreate only two or three of them at the same time. Given time, you will be able to hold all five senses in your mind at once.

THE FOURTH DAY (EVENING)

Close your eyes and perform the breathing exercises you learned on the first day. Feel and listen to your breathing. Feel the warmth or coldness of the air around your entire body. Notice the different smells in the air you breathe. Imagine how they would taste. Breathe deeply and rhythmically for a few minutes. Now imagine that the air is breathing *you* in and out.

Open your eyes and see the space around you. The space is filled with air. Close your eyes and imagine the space inside yourself. Meditate on your inner space. Imagine the space inside you is a balloon. Imagine that each time you inhale you are blowing up that balloon. With each breath it is getting bigger and bigger. Feel yourself begin to float, slowly rising. Imagine that you are moving around in the air, like a gentle breeze.

THE FIFTH DAY (MORNING)

A *koan* is a mental device used by some people to expand their sense of awareness. Koans don't make any logical sense. Indeed, they are intended to be paradoxical.

Koans are made up of words. But they defy any attempt to think about them. Do not concentrate on your koan. It expresses a state of awareness which defies the reasoning mind. It can be appreciated only through intuition. More precisely, it can be apprehended only when you share the understanding from which it sprang.

Koans are not as simple as they first appear. Most of us have lost the art of dwelling upon an idea. Yet it is this dwelling upon which is the real meditation. Remember, dwelling upon is the very opposite of thinking about. With time, your mind will learn to feel the difference between these two mental states.

By studying koans, you will develop an awareness which is different from your usual way of thinking.

There are certain levels of awareness which we cannot achieve until the brain can work in more than one way. Unlike the earlier exercises, the koan is intended to develop a more advanced awareness, not merely a keener one.

You have a choice from any one of the following koans for your morning meditation:

- What is the sound of one hand clapping?

- Monday is green.

- When I hear, I see; and when I see, I hear.

- At the beginning,
  the mountains are mountains.
  In the middle,
  the mountains are no longer mountains.
  At the end,
  the mountains are once again mountains.

- The landscape is moving;
  it is the rider who is motionless.

- You are what you are becoming;
  you are becoming what you already are.

- Find your original face.
  Discover what you were before you were born.
  Then come and show me your original face.

- Does a dog have a soul?
  No.
  Show me this nothing.

- Stop that ship on the distant horizon.

- A girl is crossing the street.
  Is she the younger or older sister?

THE FIFTH DAY (EVENING)

Choose a different koan and dwell upon it, repeating the morning exercise.

You will probably find the evening exercise easier than your first attempt in the morning. With practice, they will all become easy. With time, you will find that it is a lot of fun to make up your own koans for daily meditation.

The Way of Concentration

THE SIXTH DAY (MORNING)

Yantra is a Sanskrit word. Like a koan, a yantra is a mental device intended to increase awareness. A yantra, however, is an image on which the mind concentrates, dispelling all other thoughts. It may be an interesting stone, a picture, or anything you can see. The yantra, however, should not have too many meanings for you. In the beginning it is best if the yantra is something simple, like a cross, a circle, or a geometric design.

What is important is that the yantra you choose should be comfortable for you. What is important here as in all other forms of concentrative meditation is that you erase all thoughts but your mental device. Just gaze at your image and do nothing else.

If you do not have an image you especially want to use as your yantra, we would suggest using the geometric design at left.

THE SIXTH DAY (EVENING)

Yantra Meditation

Now that you have grasped the principle of yantric meditation, you are prepared to proceed to a more difficult phase. In this exercise, do not gaze at any physical object or image. Close your eyes and imagine your yantra. Since you must keep the image in your mind for as long as you can, choose a simple image, like the one given below.

In order to help keep your image in focus, you might rotate it in your mind. You might also let it get bigger and bigger and then smaller and smaller.

Keep your eyes closed throughout this meditation and sit very still. Concentrate very hard on the physical image before you close your eyes. In this way, the image will remain with you for a moment after you close your eyes. This will help you to focus the image in your mind's eye. If you should become distracted and lose your mental image, don't be distressed. Simply open your eyes and look at the physical image again. Then close your eyes and go back to your meditation.

THE SEVENTH DAY (MORNING)

Mantra Meditation

Mantra is another word that comes from the Sanskrit. This form of meditation is very similar to yantra meditation, except that you use a sound instead of an image as your mental device. This is the basis of the Transcendental Meditation (TM) technique, which is one of the most popular forms of meditation today.

For your mantra, you select a word or sound, such as *one, love, peace,* or even the much-used *om.* A possible difficulty, however, with choosing your own mantra is that you are apt to choose a word whose meaning or sound you like. At first, such a mantra will be helpful to you, making it easier to retain the mantra in your thoughts. In the long run, however, it may make it more difficult to practice the meditations of The Way of Negation, where even the mantra is no longer held in one's thoughts. For this reason, I suggest that you make up your own nonsense word. Any one or two syllable sound which is meaningless to you will do.

Prepare for this meditation exactly as you have for the earlier ones. When your body is completely relaxed, let your mind become aware of your breathing. Breathe through your nose, easily and naturally. Each time you breathe out, say your mantra aloud.

You may find this meditation more difficult because your mind is more subject to distractions. It's possible to even concentrate too hard on your mantra. You may eventually lose it, and stray thoughts may begin to creep into your mind. Don't let that concern you. When you become aware that you are no longer thinking your mantra, repeat the distraction to yourself three times and go back to saying your mantra.

THE SEVENTH DAY (EVENING)

The Silent Mantra
Repeat the same exercise that you did this morning—but this time don't say your mantra aloud. Repeat it silently in your mind. You will probably find that you have developed a "mental voice" and that you begin to hear the mantra. This is wrong. The mantra should be

thought, not heard. The sound of your own voice in your mind becomes a distraction.

The silent mantra should be repeated with a steady rhythm. At first you may time it with your breathing, but as your breathing slows down, try to maintain the same rhythmic repetition with which you started.

THE EIGHTH DAY (MORNING)

Mudric Meditation

A *mudra* is the repetition of your mental device with the repeated movements of your body. There are two types of mudras: stationary and active.

In the stationary mudra, you concentrate on a gesture and repeat your mantra or gaze at your yantra. The movement may be anything that is pleasing to you. It may be moving your head or hands back and forth, or watching your body as you breathe. Time your movements to the repetition of your mantra.

THE EIGHTH DAY (EVENING)

Now that you have the idea of stationary mudric meditation, you may try the more complex mudra.

This form of meditation brings together all three of the basic exercises in The Way of Meditation. Take your mantra and yantra and combine them with dance steps. Make sure that the dance steps are simple and can be repeated easily.

If you don't dance, then make up some little steps for yourself. They can be as casual as moving back and forth from one leg to another. In fact, a movement as simple as that one is often the best.

The Way of Negation

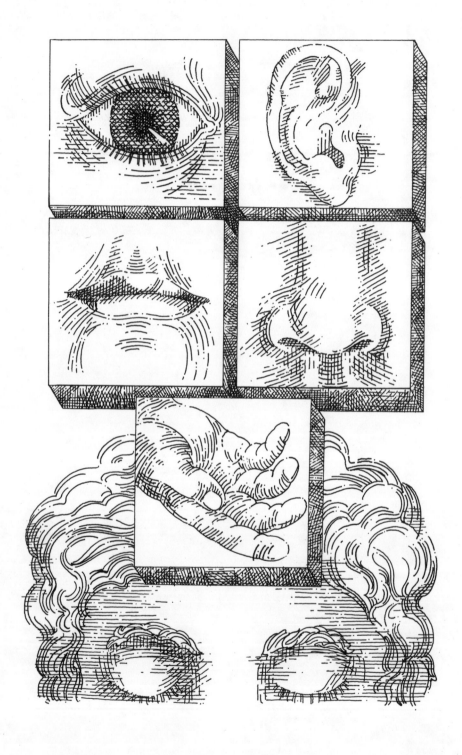

THE FIVE SENSES MEDITATION

The Way of Negation may seem opposite to The Way of Awareness and The Way of Concentration. It isn't. The Way of Negation is the invisible backbone of what you have already learned. Both of the previous Ways were an active effort to meditate upon a single thought or sensation. They were a way of letting go of distracting thoughts. This letting go is also the essence of The Way of Negation.

However, the negative way does not employ any mental device such as a mantra. It stresses "detachment" and the search for emptiness. Like The Way of Awareness or The Way of Concentration, The Way of Negation also seeks the Core of Energy.

To begin, close your eyes and relax. Imagine that you were born blind and have never seen the world around you. Imagine what that feeling must be like. Now, one by one, take away your other senses. Imagine that you can't hear anything. You have never heard any music or the sound of a human voice. Imagine that you have never tasted food. Imagine that you have never smelled anything, not even a flower.

All you have left now is your sense of touch. Imagine that you are paralyzed, that you have never felt anything. Imagine that you have lost all your senses. There is now nothing outside of your body. There is no space and no time because you cannot feel, see, hear, taste, or smell.

As you come back, add the senses one by one. Begin with your sense of feel and work your way backwards.

THE NINTH DAY (EVENING)

Begin by repeating your mantra aloud for a few minutes. Then repeat it silently for another few minutes, just as you did on the seventh day of exercises. When you reach a moment of deep concentration, let your mantra slip out of your mind. Do not let your mind be filled with other thoughts. Let your mind be empty. Dwell upon this nothingness until you feel as if you are dwelling *within* it. It is through experiencing this nothingness that you will learn to experience your Core of Energy.

These last two techniques are perhaps the most difficult of all. Repeat both these exercises in The Way of Negation for two more days, once in the morning and once in the evening. Don't be discouraged if you find this is not your Way. Instead, select that form of meditation which came to you most easily and naturally. Remember, there is no best way to meditate.

COMING OUT OF MEDITATION

The final few minutes of meditation are a swimming back to the surface. They are largely the reverse of your preparation to meditate. Relax and close your eyes (or keep them closed). Let your mind wander over your body. You will feel your muscle tone gradually restoring itself, your senses becoming alive again. Do not rush this transition. You will find it varies somewhat from session to session.

Just as you cannot will yourself into meditation, so you cannot return too quickly from a session without knowing it. With an abrupt return, your nervous system will experience a shock or discomfort.

The aftereffects of meditation will make you feel as if you have just awakened from an afternoon nap. Your relaxation, however, will have been much deeper. You will feel an unusual amount of energy and an intense alertness to everything around you.

After you have opened your eyes, remain still for a few minutes, letting your mind wander easily and naturally. You will probably find that you have moved during meditation—don't let that worry you. You will probably act as if you are waking from a deep sleep— rubbing your eyes, stretching your arms, sighing deeply, and perhaps even yawning. Let your mind and body move completely naturally. They will return of their own accord to their natural state.

After completing these exercises in meditation, you may want to share your experience with your friends. In the next chapter, we will see some of the problems and pleasures this sharing may bring.

Group
Meditation

Meditation is a private experience. Meditating alone, you can set your own pace and perform a style of meditation that suits you best. On the other hand, meditating with a friend or relative can often bring encouragement and instruction. Only you can decide which is best for you.

In group meditation, one person's needs can sometimes interfere with another's. On the other hand, group silence can make you more sensitive to other people. You may find that you draw a certain power from others, which strengthens your own meditations.

The main advantage of group meditation is that it may keep you from becoming discouraged easily. Most people become discouraged because they expect too much, too soon, with too little effort. As with any worthwhile undertaking, you must expect that there will be moments of despair. There may even be moments when you feel that you are actually growing more confused instead of achieving the calmness and clarity of mind you had hoped for.

Such moments of discouragement usually come when you are beginning to make progress. What at first seemed easy and rewarding suddenly seems completely impossible. The mind will not work. The imagination and the emotions wander away. At such times, a friend's advice and support can make all the difference.

It is probably wise to complete the exercises in this book before determining whether you should meditate with another person. At one time or another, most students of meditation will work in private as well as in a group. However, it is probably unwise to ever completely put aside private meditation. Valuable as it may be to share with others and to learn from them, you will probably learn the most from yourself.

Perhaps you already know some friends who meditate. If so, you might talk to them about meditating together. Experienced friends can be of great help to you, giving you encouragement and outside discipline. They can also steer you away from many of the pitfalls, dead-ends, and mistakes through which you would otherwise have to struggle yourself.

Nevertheless, it is certainly better to meditate alone than in a group that is wrong for you. If your meditation is alive and creative, there will be experiences which you can share and those which you cannot. The purpose of shared meditation is that people help each other in their growth. You must not set up standards for each other. If you find yourselves competing or comparing experiences, it is time to meditate alone.

Once you have completed the exercises in this book, you may want to set up your own meditation group. If you do, you must expect to be asked the same questions you asked yourself when you were beginning.

Questions
and Answers

Of all the questions students ask about meditation, probably the most frequently asked is "Will meditation help me to learn faster?"

The answer is "Definitely." Tests of those who meditate and those who do not showed that meditators had much better memories. This was true for both their ability to remember recent events and those long since passed.

Such experiments tend to confirm the opinion that the mind absorbs everything, like a sponge. The problem of learning is really one of remembering what we have learned.

Another question which people
frequently ask is "Will
meditation change my personality?"

Your personality may change—and probably for the better. But apart from feeling less tense, there will probably be few changes which you will notice yourself. A usual experience with meditators is that they become discouraged after a few months because they feel nothing is happening. Then one day someone will say to them, "You've really changed!" The personality changes which occur are very subtle. They will be much more apparent to other people than they will be to you.

"What is the difference between
the various styles of meditation
and the experience of meditation?"

The styles or techniques of meditation remain unchanged from session to session. Meditation, however, is a continuing experience and provides the meditator with ceaseless chances for change and inner growth.

"What will I be conscious
of when I meditate?"

You will enter into a state of *pure consciousness.* This is the final goal of all forms of meditation. When you allow your attention to shift inward, you will experience quiet levels of the mind in which you become more and more aware. Meditation consists of nothing more than being wide awake inside without being aware of anything except awareness itself.

"Won't I become discouraged
after the first few weeks of
meditation and give it up?"

With every young meditator, there will be frequently recurring periods of mental laziness. Such moments are usually the result of having over-extended yourself or meditating incorrectly. These moments of discouragement will continue to come until you establish a state of balance between your life and the new experience which has entered into it.

"What is this balance and
how will I achieve it?"

This balance comes about when the higher consciousness, which you achieved during meditation, has established itself as the governing force in your life. With repeated meditation, you remake, transform, and unify yourself and your life. With all the tensions now gone from your mind and body, you have freed a large amount of energy which must now be put to some practical purpose.

"What does the meditation
experience feel like?"

This question is almost always asked and it is almost impossible to answer. Most meditators try to answer by expressing the "sense of oneness" that they feel. During meditation, they feel "at one" with themselves and the world around them.

It requires a great deal of imagination to understand this answer, but it is one of the better descriptions of meditation which we have. But you should not be content with such descriptions. You will find it easier to answer the question for yourself—by beginning to meditate right now.

Index